To *The Bri* from *The Babe* with love.
Brian changed our lives bringing fun into our world.

To my four, forever loved, children Dan, Rae, Matt and Becky. You were the reason behind those 39 jobs.

And to all the amazing characters I met over the years – without you there would be no memoir.

Finally, Becky, Daren, Logan and Amber (The Redstone/Bales) and Kerry Smith. Five very special people. Special and important in my life.

GAY REDSTONE

Fangs for the Memory

39 JOBS IN 55 YEARS

50% of the profits from each book sold will be donated to the Loughborough Rainbows Hospice for Children and Young People

Published by Goldcrest Books International Ltd
www.goldcrestbooks.com
publish@goldcrestbooks.com

ISBN: 978-1-913719-26-5
eISBN: 978-1-913719-27-2

Illustrations: Gay Redstone

INTRODUCTION

How best to tell you the story of my working life? Shall I call it *Time Travel, A Journey of 39 Steps*, or *Fangs for the Memory?*

From 1954 to 2009, aged 15 to 70, I had in excess of 39 jobs.

By taking you on this journey I will tell you of people I met on the way – stories amazing, amusing and kindnesses shown. All of them are true, as far as my memory allows.

Thrown into the mix will be modes of transport to the places of employment, and the social life of those early days.

In my memoir, I seem to go off on a tangent, this is because I am looking back and telling stories related to me by others, their memories then become part of my memory bank. Sadly, many of the people I write about are no longer with us.

My memory fails me of wages earned; some remembered, most not.

Enjoy travelling with me. My promise – this will not be boring!

PART 1

The Early Years

Stead and Simpson, aged 15, 1954

Leaving Roundhill Secondary Modern School, Thurmaston in 1954, aged 15, I had no qualifications, no confidence and few expectations. Unable to spell and with a poor memory I believed myself to be stupid. It was many years before dyslexia was diagnosed, and how that knowledge changed my life!

I was interested in becoming a hairdresser, also, I would have liked to have worked with children, but back in 1954 you did what your parents dictated and office work paid a higher wage than trainee hairdressing or child care, so I became an office clerk at Stead and Simpson, boot and shoe manufacturers, working with figures – no spelling!

As junior clerk, my remit was to go around the warehouse several times a day, collecting invoices from the various departments. With the name Gay, and 15 years old, I was teased and likened to well-known race horses at that time – Gay's the Word, and Gay Trip – how times and meanings have changed.

My boss, Mr Colin Jackman, a quiet, shy and unassuming man, would just frown at me on my return for sometimes taking longer than I should have; yes, I was a chatterbox – still am!

A fascinating fact: One of the departments I collected invoices from was the hosiery department. It was a small unit, with perhaps half-a-dozen ladies, who were fully occupied mending ladders in nylon stockings sent in by customers through Stead and Simpson's 240 retail shops around the country. Hard for us to imagine now, mending ladders in nylon stockings – no miniskirts, and no tights just yet. The statue of the little Victorian girl outside the City Rooms on Hotel Street, Leicester, is doing the same job, but no synthetic fibres.

I remember Mr Harry Gee, a director at Stead and Simpson's. He always acknowledged you if he passed you in the street by raising his bowler hat – even to me at 15 – that meant so much.

At 16, and striving for pastures new, I started working at W H Lea's, a large family department store on the corner of Charles Street and Humberstone Gate, and near the Bell Hotel in Leicester. I was an assistant in the gown department – ladies' dresses and outer wear. I left after six weeks – too much competition fighting over customers. I liked the job but not the atmosphere.

What next? Why had I left Stead and Simpson? I was happy there; perhaps they would take me back?

Talking to my old boss, Mr Jackman, he said, 'I'm sorry, your old job isn't available.'

I was just thinking, serves me right imagining they would think of taking me back, when Mr Jackman said: 'But we do have a vacancy that you could fill, and it carries a pay rise.'

So, I was back with a promotion and a pay rise. I stayed until I was 18.

***

All my working life I made friends who came to be lifelong friends. I worked with Barbara Knights, who was 18 to my 15, and we became close friends.

In those days, Stead and Simpson's office closed for lunch from 12.30 until 2.00 p.m. On sunny days Barbara and I would walk straight down Church Gate – there was no Vaughan Way or St Margaret's Way then – into Abbey Park and to the lake where we would hire a rowing boat for an hour. Barbara would row one time and me the next and we would walk back to the office for 2.00 p.m.

Everyone thought we were crazy, but it was fun and preferable to wandering around the shops.

However, some days we did mooch around the shops in our lunch break. One day we were trying on hats in Marks & Spencer's; there were dozens of hats displayed on large tables – we wore hats back in the late 50s. I put my hat down and tried on several. There was nothing I liked, but by this time someone

was walking towards the till with my hat in her hand!
What an embarrassing moment.

Over seventy years later, in 2019, I was at M&S in
Fosse Park, Leicester, looking for a new jacket. That
season's colours, browns and beiges, were not to my
taste except for one jacket that was a gorgeous powder
blue. It was off the rail and on my back before you
could say 'one o'clock'.

'Excuse me,' a red-faced lady said, 'that's my jacket.'

I apologised profusely and we both laughed about
it. I did say: 'Why are you looking for another jacket
when this is the nicest one in the store?'

'This is summer-weight; I'm looking for winter-
weight,' she replied.

Oh well, no new jacket for me that day. I'm sure
there's a moral here: do not covet ...

***

Occasionally, and with snow on the ground, a group
of us would walk to the pavilion in Abbey Park. I
remember drinking hot chocolate and I think there
was possibly a log fire (but that might be a trick of the
memory). What I do remember is the beauty of the
park, decked in snow – magic.

Many years later, Barbara and Colin Jackman
married. They remained lifelong friends of mine.

While I was at Stead and Simpson I also had Saturday
jobs, first at C&A Modes, which was then situated on
Granby Street; a building I'm guessing between Dover
Street and York Street. Later, and with my close friend,
Brenda, I worked a Saturday job at the Boulevard Café
on Market Street in Loughborough, serving snacks and

espresso coffee. Students and shoppers would come in for said coffee and snacks, and sometimes coffee and toast, literally just one slice of toast, buttered and cut 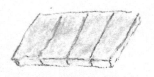 into soldiers, but sometimes two slices. Would that happen now? We would be slimmer, that's for sure.

Modes of transport to the city

While at Stead and Simpson I would catch the 7.30 a.m. bus from Cossington. I would know most passengers and the ladies would all knit and natter.

Summer months would see me cycling to work – Cossington to Mansfield Street in Leicester was quite a trek. On my journey home, Mr Chaplin, Brenda's father, who was also cycling, would sometimes catch me up. He would place one hand in the small of my back and I would sail up the hills – what a treat!

Richmond House, aged 18 to 24, 1957 to 1963

Gay at 18, taken when she worked at
Richmond House.

Richmond House was the clinic for Leicester City schools. It was situated in the Newarke, directly behind the Art and Technical College, and side by side with Gateway Boys' School. Richmond House was a beautiful period house but is sadly no more. It has been replaced by a modern building – how was that allowed to happen?

I was employed as a telephonist and used the old board with 'eyelids' and a wind-up handle. I remember someone coming from the telephone exchange to train me. Amazingly, there was also someone employed to come and disinfect the mouthpiece!

I soon found out that to be a mind reader would be an asset in this job.

Example:

'Can I speak to Miss Waters, please?'

'I'm sorry, we don't have a Miss Waters working here.'

'Yes, Dear, Miss Waters. She makes the eye clinic appointments.'

'Oh,' I said, 'you mean Miss Pool.'

'Yes, Dear, that's what I said, Miss Pool.'

'Hold the line, I'm putting you through.'

As one of the junior members of the office it would sometimes be my job to fetch the filled cobs from a little shop in a row on the corner of Millstone Lane and Oxford Street, and on someone's birthday, to fetch cakes from Elizabeth the Chef in Halford Street – mostly cream cakes; very expensive and very yummy.

One weekly task with an office mate, another Barbara, was to collect the staff wages from Head Office in Newarke Street, with Mr Clarke from the appointment's office following at a safe distance.

This particular cold morning we passed a group of workmen, who were drinking tea and warming their hands around a fire. One of us remarked on this but slipped up on the word brazier, calling it a brassiere and then realising the mistake. We fell about laughing. Brazier – brassiere – they wish!

That afternoon we were summoned to the boss's office (Mr Frank Timpson) and told to calm down or he would send someone else. We calmed down.

Can you imagine teenagers walking down the street today carrying cash wages for twenty people? Why didn't they just send Mr Clarke, or a different couple, each week? The minds of men!

Richmond House was a brilliant place to work alongside doctors, nurses and school dentists, and it was here that I met Lilian Measures. Her hobby was singing, as was mine. I was 18, Lilian was in her late 50s. We became very close and Lilian was my 'surrogate mum', and at around 64 she became godmother to Daniel, my firstborn. Lilian worried that she was too old to take on that role. She lived to be 84.

After a couple of years I was promoted and became clerk to Sister Betty Hunt, the ENT (Ear, Nose and Throat) Nurse, sending out appointments for her clinics and travelling with her to city primary schools where I assisted her with the audiometry testing of children's hearing.

Sister Hunt was very strict and outspoken; she could be quite intimidating. We travelled to all of the schools by city bus, and I got to see a different side to

Sister Hunt. I loved being her clerk and worked with her until I left in 1963 to start a family. I got to know all the school doctors and nurses and learnt some interesting stories.

Doctor Isidor Dub (as in tube) would always raise his bowler hat if meeting you in the street, but would almost trip, organising his briefcase and umbrella, in order to raise his hat. He was a jolly man who would regale us with stories of his escape from war-torn Europe (Dr Dub was Jewish) and stated that he was never sure what he was most terrified of; being stopped or the fear he felt when travelling on the back of a friend's motorcycle. Dr Dub was married to Trudie Dub, a well-known local author.

I remember a beautiful, Boston Ivy-clad Victorian house on London Road, opposite Victoria Park, the home of one of the clinic's doctors, which was sadly demolished in the 1960s and replaced with a modern, square, office-block. How sad. So many beautiful buildings were lost at that time.

One of the perks of working for the City Council was being selected as poll clerks, or vote counters for local and General Elections. I enjoyed both but preferred the count in the evenings. They were originally at Granby Halls and then later at De Montfort Hall. There was quite a buzz as the results filtered through, and tension when there had to be re-counts if the votes were too close or disputed. These were always watched closely by the tellers and party supporters, and in the case of re-counts, didn't finish until the small hours. The pay, which was generous, was in addition to our normal wages – quite an incentive!

***

For a while it was on the bus at 7.30 a.m. with the knit and natter group, then I had a brainwave – I could either cycle to Rothley, leave my bike at a friend's house, and catch the Loughborough to Leicester bus at the Halfway House pub (Dimbleby's – later the Red Lion and now Miller & Carter) and many a time getting a lift in a friend's car (thanks Derek). Or, I could cycle to Sileby, throw my bike into the shed at the back of the pork butcher's shop, sprint up the steps to the station platform just as the train was invariably screeching to a halt. All of this to give me half an hour extra in bed!

Travelling by train was so much fun. Back in the day several of us would manage to get a carriage together – an eight-seater compartment, not quite steam trains. Often, we would play card games, have heated discussions, a lot of laughter and quite a lot of falling in and out of love with fellow travellers. Aah, memories!

Brenda and I had imaginary friends. Yes, sadly, at 18 years old! I was going to tell you about our travelling companion; then I wasn't – too silly I thought, then I was – I will explain.

In 1939 T. S. Eliot, in his poetry book *Old Possum's Book of Practical Cats*, had a character called Skimbleshanks the railway cat, and in 1957, Brenda and Gay created a three-inch-tall travelling companion called Dumpledinks. Forty years later, in 1997, J. K. Rowling, in her first Harry Potter book, created Professor Dumbledore, Head of Hogwarts School of Wizardry – Skimbleshanks, Dumpledinks, Dumbledore – the only silly thing was, our creation didn't become famous. Sorry Dumpledinks.

Dumpledinks

Dumpledinks only travelled,
on the Loughborough to Leicester line.
On the days he travelled,
the train would be on time.

Dumple chose with whom he would travel,
loved a problem to help unravel.
We would listen with admiration,
as problem solved before Syston station.

He will join you in a tic,
and leave again, just as quick.
Always full of fun – a happy little chap,
in the words of Forest Gump, 'that's all I have to say
about that.'

Having arrived at London Road Station, we would go our separate ways. Most of our group worked at the County Hall offices on the corner of Greyfriars and Friar Lane. I would walk along Belvoir Street, Newarke Street, through the Magazine archway into The Newarke by Magazine Square, the old army drill yard, and at some point in the day talk to an elderly lady – the last widow still living in the married quarters that surrounded the Square – and into Richmond Street and work.

Lunchtime meant meeting friends in town; this time walking along Millstone Lane and Horsefair Street to meet under Kemp's clock, close to the entrance to the market, or at Bruccaini's if the weather was inclement. You would find us standing at tall tables, no stools, drinking coffee or hot chocolate – a wonderful meeting venue.

Sunny days would find us in Town Hall Square, picnicking on the grass – dozens of people.

Once a week a couple of us would walk along New Walk for the lunchtime concerts at the New Walk Museum (now renamed Leicester Museum and Art Gallery). Small groups of musicians played classical music – a grand piano, violin, classical guitar, mainly for the university students.

If we were going to the cinema in the week we would stay in town after work and go for something to eat. Remember the Regency Café on Cheapside back in the 1950s? There were no fast-food places; you could get a good meal really cheaply and then go to the cinema, running for the 10.00 p.m. Leicester to Loughborough bus via Cossington and Sileby afterwards.

Saturday night would almost always see us out dancing; usually Brenda and me. Our favourite haunts in Leicester were De Montfort Hall, the Art and Technical College, the Bell Hotel and occasionally the Fire Station on Lancaster Road. The Palais, from time to time, was reserved for special occasions and the Bell Hotel tended to be a slightly older, more sophisticated group.

I had dancing lessons at the Empress Ballroom on London Road, a tiny studio with a sprung floor, so I could comfortably dance the waltz, foxtrot and quickstep. We probably went to De Montfort Hall more frequently than other dance halls and because I'd had dancing lessons I was able to attract other dancers. Brenda hadn't taken dance lessons but neither of us were ever wallflowers.

An interesting story, typical of the 1950s

Being able to dance meant that I was never without a partner and would get to know these partners.

A very attractive Asian Indian young man was a frequent partner. I remember having romantic thoughts about him! We had a warm relationship, only ever meeting up at De Montfort Hall. I knew in my heart that my parents – who I had a difficult relationship with – would have banished me, and I always avoided conflict. Well, I have to tell you he never asked me out, and I suspect he would have had similar problems with his own family. I was always happy if our paths crossed. That probably wouldn't happen today – times have changed, fortunately.

From time to time a group of us from Sileby and Cossington would go to a dance in Syston, travelling there by bus but having a taxi pick us up around 11.30 p.m. The taxi ride was usually the highlight of our evening and quite hysterical. The taxi owner would only do one journey – he must have worked in a sardine factory for the taxi became a sardine tin on wheels. How he managed to pack us all in!

Brenda and I, although very close, had totally different hobbies and interests. Brenda was very artistic and attended art classes. More sporty than me, Brenda loved playing tennis.

My main hobby was singing and from around eight years old I have always found a choir to belong to. The first serious choir was when I was fifteen, The Midland Music Lovers Choir, Sileby, singing at music festivals all over the Midlands. I have even sung tenor in Ladies' Barbershop!

I believe singing has been my saviour through difficult times in my life, and at eighty-one I still sing with the Newtown Linford Choral Society, and as well as through my working life, I made many lifelong friends through singing.

The one time I persuaded Brenda to join me in singing was to an augmented choir – Loughborough Schools and Churches singing Handel's *Messiah*. Often Keith says that all of her life Brenda loved that oratorio and would stop whatever she was doing to sing along whenever she heard it.

We did both love cycling and youth hostelled together several times in the West Country. Memories!

***

Living in the country had its drawbacks – we would take all afternoon to get ready, then put a headscarf tightly on our heads to hold our hair in place, while we cycled to Rothley.

One foggy night the new boyfriend was picking me up at 7.30 p.m. for a 'posh' dinner dance at the Grand Hotel. My train was delayed and I didn't get home until 8.00 p.m. and said boyfriend was sitting in my parents' living room. Can you imagine the total embarrassment of me then carrying a bucket of hot water through the living room and up to my bedroom to wash and get ready? There was no bathroom and the toilet was down the garden, no mobiles, in fact, no phones. Not the best start for a relationship with an up-and-coming trainee accountant!

Did we appreciate how carefree our lives were through those years? Of course not, we knew no different.

PART 2

Oadby and Marriage

In 1959, aged 20, I was courting Ken and for many years we were programme sellers at De Montfort Hall, getting paid and getting to see concerts for free!

Ken and I married in 1961 and our first home together was a 1930s semi in Grosvenor Crescent, Oadby – it cost £1,600. Our mortgage was £8 per month and my income was not taken into account. A mortgage at that time was a quarter of the man's monthly income. Even so, this was the start of some very lean years and the progress of my story – 39 jobs!

***

In 1963 I left Richmond House; our first child was due in the September. Having been adopted myself, Daniel was so special, he was the first thing that truly belonged to me. Rachel was born seventeen months later – why was I disappointed? Because I only wanted boys. I loved her but it was three months before I understood that I was afraid that because of the poor relationship with my adoptive mother that history might repeat itself. I remember picking Rachel up, cuddling her and saying, 'Everything's going to be all right,' and it was, we had a wonderful relationship.

Money was tight and my determination to be a stay-at-home mum presented challenges. We would take in lodgers and we started with the D'oyly Carte Opera

Company. That was a practice run – no payment but complimentary tickets.

Our lodgers were usually theatre actors, or technicians from travelling theatres. Can anyone remember the Living Theatre who performed in the old St Nicholas School Rooms, 1960–1963? The Living Theatre left Leicester when in 1963 productions moved to the Phoenix Theatre. Our lodgers at that time came from the Phoenix, now the Sue Townsend Theatre.

One lovely man, I would say in his thirties, stayed with us for a while. His name was Leonard Fenton. Later, and for many years, Leonard was Dr Legg in Eastenders. When he left us he gave us a beautiful book, *Mayhew's London*, signed by Leonard. It was an account of Victorian London; the costermongers, the early theatre. Sadly, that lovely book was lost during a house clearance in 2016. If anyone comes across it …

One time I did 'out work' at home, covering buttons with fabric. I usually worked in the evening, standing at a little machine that was clamped to a kitchen surface. Unfortunately, I was good at what I did, being very particular that each button was correct. Why unfortunate? Well, Aubrey, my boss, would bring me all his samples to make up. Now, if he paid me 3d per dozen normally, he would pay me 6d (5p) per dozen for the samples, which, trust me, took far longer than twice as long.

I became a childminder in 1967; two of our own, Daniel, four and Rachel, two, and my friend Florence's son, Simon, also aged two. I purchased a second-hand twin pushchair, a side-by-side one, and could be seen walking miles with the three children strapped in.

Over the years we spent hour upon hour in the Botanic Gardens in Oadby. The entrance back in the 1960s was Hastings House, on Stoughton Drive South – opposite to where we lived; now it's Glebe House on Glebe Road. To us it was the students' gardens as that's where some of the residential university students lived.

A promise of being good while I did the chores resulted in a picnic in the gardens, often just a pile of sandwiches, a big bottle of squash and plastic beakers. We could spend two to three hours playing around the large lily pond with all its fish, the Elizabethan Knot garden – a sunken garden surrounded by highly perfumed box hedges, and walk ways covered with climbing roses and clematis. Apart from the gardeners, who we got to know, we would see no one else. We even knew which large stone to remove to reveal a tap that turned on a little fountain in the lily pond. We used to turn it on when we arrived and always remembered to turn it off again as we left. That has all changed now and a large bell sits where the little fountain used to be.

I tell you these stories because we didn't have much money and these beautiful gardens cost us nothing to visit.

Years later, and living in Anstey, the students' gardens were regularly visited, now with Becky and friends.

I remember taking six children strawberry picking with another mum, and never understood why the farmers didn't weigh the children in and out, as their half-full punnets, and the tell-tale vision of red stains down their t-shirts, told their own story!

Around this time I became an Avon lady, and later, evenings again, Party Plan with Sarah Coventry jewellery and other Party Plan products, and finally Tupperware. I'm still using some Tupperware pieces from that time and I still have wine and sherry glasses that were prizes in an Avon promotion.

Through the 1960s we were very much into Party Plan. I remember Just Jacqui starting back in the 60s with Party Plan. She had an amazing taste in gorgeous, affordable outfits – very popular with us young mums. Later, Jacqui opened a high-class ladies' gown shop on Welford Road and was there for many years.

Stainless steel parties were very popular, and beautiful pottery made by Valerie Blease. I still have a round pottery cheese platter, with an adorable little mouse with a very upturned nose. It's so cute and I only every use it for blue Stilton cheese!

Blue Stilton? Oh no-se!

In 1975-ish my close friends were Jan and Tony Clay – Jan an executive manager with Tupperware, Tony an able assistant. I was in Jan's team, which brings on a story.

We were staying in Oadby waiting for our mortgage to come through for 5 Highfield Street, Anstey, (more about that later). Tony, Jan and I were going to a Tupperware meeting. Tony had taken three beefsteaks out of the freezer to defrost for our meal later. You've guessed – as it defrosted the dog got a whiff of it and that was the end of supper. The air was blue, our dog, Gipsy, flew through the back door, and me? I decided to have an early night!

***

In 1968 we adopted Matthew. I was adopted myself and wanted to give something back, so with three children, and still determined not to work full-time, I started working night shifts at the Leicester Royal Infirmary as an auxiliary nurse. There was no actual nursing involved, but I got good with the bed pans! When night shifts, and little sleep during the day, became too much, and by now the children were at school or playgroup, I did domestic cleaning jobs.

Wendy Bairstow, who lived in Oadby, had advertised for domestic help. Wendy was a delight to work for, often leaving me cleaning but also listening out for the baby while she popped out for a while. On her return, she would often find me cuddling baby Neil, changing his nappy or giving him a bottle, and Wendy would be sure that I'd kicked his cot to waken him!

Another cleaning job, and the lady of the house would totally ignore me, even to the point of walking into the kitchen, me on my hands and knees scrubbing the floor, and turn on the radio when she entered and turning it off again when she left. Hello! Mr Cellophane from the musical *Chicago* comes to mind. I didn't stay there long, and strangely, I cannot remember her name.

When all three children were at school I worked in the school kitchen for a time. It was very busy and hard work; all those baking tins and trays to be hand-washed. When the kitchen was pristine and ready for the next day we would sit down for our dinner. I loved school dinners.

Traffic counts also kept a little extra money coming in, the counting done by five-bar gates – IIII IIII – and in later years we had to press a button on a hand-held machine – progress!

***

In 1969 I trained to be a telephonist at the telephone exchange on Wharf Street (Leicester GPO) – the first job I was ever properly trained for. I loved that job and was gaining confidence in my own ability, as I began to understand that I had a condition called dyslexia, which had nothing to do with intelligence, or lack of it.

A particular area that I enjoyed working on was Directory Enquiries. Before the computer age and using only telephone directories from each part of Great Britain, we were trained to find a number anywhere in the country in 60 seconds. So your duties would be 'A' boards or directories – 'A' boards were for connecting calls (there were very few automatic exchanges back in the 1970s) and only four-digit numbers, for example, MH4853, MM8534, LU5843, HK3854. Including area codes, they are eleven-digit numbers now.

Memories of how few callers there were when the 'soaps' were on – Coronation Street, Emmerdale Farm (the first episode was in October 1972). Remember the Forsythe Saga, 1968/69? With 18 million viewers our boards would go silent until ... and then, wow! Did we make up for the quiet time! The National Grid had problems with the sudden surge of electricity needed: lights, kettles, cookers, telephones, all of a sudden in use again.

Sadly, while this job was so good in that it built my confidence and self-belief, it also saw the end of our marriage. We had grown apart and started to live separate lives.

PART 3

A New Life

Having spent my teenage years in Cossington, a north Leicestershire village, I was very familiar with the district, regularly cycling, usually with Brenda, to Bradgate Park, Mount St Bernard's Abbey and the surrounding area. A picnic in the park with the chaplain's family could take up most of the day – all of us on bikes!

Now I found myself and the children renting a house in Anstey. I really felt I was coming home.

We all settled quickly into village life. I remember Matthew (Matt), aged six, coming in from school saying: 'I'm off to play with cousin Jem.'

'Okay,' I said, 'but why did you say cousin Jem? Jeremy isn't your cousin.'

'Well,' he said, 'everyone else has cousins.' How true.

Anstey, unlike Oadby, was made up with two, three, four, and even five, generation families. You had to be careful not to say the wrong thing! So cousin Jem it was.

Rachel, (Rae) was busy, busy, busy making new friends and loving the freedom of village life.

Daniel, (Danny) an animal lover, was already rising at 5.30 a.m. and off to bring the cows in for milking for an elderly, local farmer, Mr Sibson. Danny would ride on an ancient, sit-up-and-beg bike, which was kept in the yard for the purpose.

I got a part-time job, driving for the Langrop garage in Anstey, fetching cars in for their servicing and MOTs, and driving to town to pick up parts.

I did manage to write a car off for them – one of theirs, fortunately. Travelling along Anstey Lane towards Anstey, just before Roydene Crescent, the car in front of me, without indicating, braked sharply to turn right into Roydene Crescent. I braked but crashed into the rear of his car and the car following crashed into my car – three very damaged cars, and mine, of course, much worse. I was petrified as to what Langrop's would say. Whoever I told just said, 'Don't worry about it, we're insured, I wrote one off last week.'

One time, on my 9.00 a.m. to 1.00 p.m. shift, they sent me up to Sheffield to pick up an urgent part. I manged it, of course. I loved driving a decent car, but worried that I was responsible for three young children, so I moved on.

I had to work and needed a job urgently. My friend Derek phoned me with several vacancies that had arisen at County Hall – I attended for an interview. I explained to the two ladies from personnel that, being dyslexic, I had problems with spelling and memory. Smiling, one of them said, 'Gay, you're not exactly selling yourself to us.'

'No,' I replied, 'but I am being honest and it would be no good to either of us offering me a job I can't cope with. What I can say is that I'm hard-working, conscientious and a good team player.'

They offered me a position in the Education Post Room – perfect!

My overall boss of Transport and Communications was Mr Geoff Prattley. My immediate boss of the post room was Liz Jarvis. She, and her husband, Tom, were to become lifelong friends.

A couple of heart-warming stories

After working in the post room for just one week I was shocked to realise that we were paid monthly. How was I, with no savings, to manage paying the rent and feed the children? I talked to Mr Prattley asking him if he thought staff-wages accounts might be able to help in some way.

'No,' he said, 'I doubt they can, but no problem, I will lend you what you need and you can pay me back over several months.' No written agreement, just trust. I remember crying with relief.

Thank you, Geoff, I will never forget your kindness to me, and I never have.

Another kindness story

After a couple of years I bought an old banger – a B registration Hillman Imp in two-tone navy blue and rust. Not altogether reliable.

Jack, a driver for the City Council, would come each day with post for us. Four of us in the post room became friends and if he timed it right, he would have a tea break with us.

I was about to take the children to visit friends in Norfolk – 'cousin' Jem and his family were now living near Mundesley – but wondering if that would be foolish in such a clapped-out rust bucket.

On the Monday morning, Jack came along telling us that he had bought a new car over the weekend.

'I will sell my old car but will hang on to it for two to three weeks before doing so.' He looked at me, 'so, Gay, you can borrow it. Get it insured for two weeks and it's yours for the holiday.'

How wonderfully kind was that? There's so much goodness in the world.

We had a safe and wonderful holiday.

***

That first Christmas on our own was going to be tough. No Christmas tree, no money to buy one – no complaining – we would improvise and make our own decorations.

A few days before Christmas a tree was delivered, a gift from a lady I had worked with. The same day a letter arrived in the post enclosing a £10 note and a cryptic clue – a gift of £10 was a fortune in the 70s. Thank you Brenda and Keith. So many special people in my life.

That Christmas I made a new rule: Santa presents could be opened as usual when everyone was awake, but the tree presents were not to be opened until after dinner; three to four o'clock.

The children declared me the meanest mother ever!

At around eleven o'clock a deputation of three arrived in the kitchen.

'Mum, can we open just one present each from under the tree?'

'Good idea,' I said, 'just one each.'

Twelve o'clock – 'Mum, just one more?'

One o'clock – 'Mum, just one more?'

This continued until dinner at three o'clock, each gift having been carefully looked at and played with.

Surprise! The following year the children asked if they could do the same again. They told their friends that this was our family tradition.

Do you remember Colin and Barbara, Stead and Simpson's, back in the 1950s? They were now married and living in Glenfield and had become lifelong friends. That same Christmas they invited me and the children to spend the whole day with them on Boxing Day. The children had had 'new' bikes for Christmas, so I walked and they rode to Salcombe Drive, Glenfield. None of us adults were drinkers, but Barbara and Colin had brought cherry brandy back from a trip abroad. They plied me with drink, none of us being aware of its strength – I thought it was lovely. I finished up being helped onto a bed to sleep off my stupor, while Barbara and Colin entertained my children until I was sober enough to walk back to Anstey with them. The children had a fantastic time, and me, well I was still on that steep learning curve.

***

Now working at County Hall I would have a small order of groceries delivered each week. On 12 September 1975, I realised I was ordering seven tins of dog food every week – the highest cost items on my order and one I could not easily afford. Yes, we'd acquired a dog that I couldn't afford. Did I have a choice? You decide.

One evening each week after work I would take the children to swim at the Holiday Inn on St Nicholas Circle in Leicester's city centre. In the early evening we would always be the only people there; the cost being a pot of tea, a plate of biscuits and three Coca Colas. I never went in the pool but relaxed with my tea and a book while the children swam. We loved it. It was on such an evening during a summer holiday that we returned home around 9.00 p.m. to find a beautiful dog lying in the road outside our house. It would not budge. I cooked a swift supper, a sausage and bacon grill, which mostly got fed to the dog – we put it on our garden wall to entice him off the road. We have always believed that he was dumped from a car.

Opening the back door at 6.30 a.m. the following day, there was the dog. This went on for a few days, the children pleading that we should keep him and me adamant that we couldn't, wouldn't, shouldn't.

I spoke to a police officer who explained that the animal centre would keep a dog for so many weeks and if it's not claimed or rehomed the animal would be put down (I believe times have changed).

'Oh, no,' I said, 'he may be a stray but he is a beautiful dog.'

'Madam,' he said, in a very patient voice, 'they put down Great Danes.'

I thanked him and put down the 'phone, and, talking aloud to myself: 'Well, girl, you have just got yourself a dog!'

Gipsy became our much-loved dog, and if we had done him a kindness, then he repaid us a hundred times. He died when he was 17 years old. Did I have a choice?

Gipsy was not a pedigree, neither was he 'Heinz 57' – he was more golden retriever than anything. In another life he would have made a very successful escapologist! Whenever we moved in Anstey he would visit the old neighbours, who loved and encouraged him. He knew to cross the village centre (The Nook) by the crossing but never quite got the hang of waiting for the lights to change. Not the way to keep a dog, I hear you say, and I agree. We keep dogs differently now, but we're talking about Gipsy – a travelling man, a free spirit, a law unto himself – and it became apparent that he had 'hostages to fortune' around the village.

As he got older he would spend hours sitting or lying on our neighbour, Colin's, lawn. We knew they were close but what we didn't realise was that most days Gipsy travelled from Anstey to the General Hospital and waited in the car while Colin visited his mother. He had his own rug and this went on for weeks, apparently, sitting in the passenger seat – a companion. What a dog!

One day, I took ill at work and was brought home from County Hall. I went straight to bed. Gipsy followed me up the stairs (not normally allowed) and as quick as a flash, he laid alongside my shaking body, absolutely still, and his eyes said, 'Let me stay here and I will get you warm' – and he did.

There were other instances like that where he watched out for us and looked after us.

***

I was happy at County Hall, paid well, but money was still a little tight, so I fell back on taking in lodgers as a small extra income.

The Haymarket theatre opened in 1973. A guy who was working as a technician at the Haymarket stayed for a couple of weeks. He would come in really late after a performance and cook supper for himself – that was the arrangement, mine was just a B&B. I would stand chatting to him, fascinated by the fact that he used one frying pan, one fork and a plate for the whole operation – I can use every knife, fork and spoon to make a cake.

A rep., who travelled in magazines, stayed for three to four months. He was very popular with the children as he kept them supplied with comics. He stayed Sunday to Thursday evening. I heard him come in late one Sunday – stairs, bathroom, bedroom door shut. On Monday morning I cooked his breakfast, which was always a large fry-up. Following the normal routine, one of the children would take coffee to him: 'Breakfast nearly ready.'

His bedroom was empty, bed not slept in. What had I heard?

We lived in a semi and evidently it had been the man next door. I'd heard him quite clearly through the wall.

As the children and I usually only had toast and cereal, I had never seen a meal devoured so quickly by three hungry mouths!

I was to take in one more lodger, but more about that later.

***

Working full-time at County Hall, and earning a decent wage, it occurred to me that I might be able to get a mortgage and buy my own place. I found that on my income I could support an £8,000 mortgage. The monthly repayments would be less than the rent I was paying, so I went for it.

We wanted to stay in the village and I found a beautifully modernised three-storey, old terraced house on Highfield Street, Anstey for £6,500, enabling me to have full central heating installed and the through-lounge/diner carpeted.

My solicitor, John Waite, declared that I was his first female client to have a mortgage in her own right – no male guarantor – yet it had been only the previous year that I'd had to have a male guarantor to rent a television.

Times were changing at last!

***

I was into DIY and a friend had given me an old Ercol table and four chairs – after my shocked reaction when she told me that she was going to paint the table white and put it in the garden.

I stripped and re-varnished that lovely table and used it daily for the next ten-plus years, then *I* gave it away to help another friend in need.

Another friend had a very lucrative side-line – he bought old, but painted, pine furniture, stripped the pieces back to bare wood, and every couple of weeks he would take a van-load off to one of the London markets and make a fortune.

Fortunately for me, some of the items he stripped

down were not pine, and not suitable for the London market. He would sell them off locally, so cheaply, just to get rid of them. I gathered quite an eclectic mix that made us a lovely home.

Our own place! How we loved it.

I decided that the children should have their own house-warming party. We designed and made the invitations ourselves.

At County Hall I'd got to know a young couple who ran their own disco – the Mistron Disco. We had a through-lounge and I booked them for the evening and requested them to bring some music and *all* their flashing lights. We set up a soft drinks bar – bad example? Perhaps – and of course, food.

The age range was 8-14 and those kids had a ball. I remember a 9-year-old asking *me* for a dance! And at 9.30 p.m. the disco couple dashed out to get more soft drinks to keep the party swinging. What a fantastic memory for all of us.

The following week the children stayed over with their dad and I had my own house-warming – our own music and no flashing lights. It was a very successful evening, except, I bit into a crusty cob and broke a crown on a front tooth leaving behind a stump.

Come Monday morning I rang Mr Prattley (Geoff) explaining that I was going straight to my dentist's on London Road, Leicester, and would get into the office as soon as possible – no need to talk to anyone on the way. Well, that didn't go to plan; the car broke down on Frog Island (remember, no mobile phones) so now I did have to speak to people. I walked into the reception area of a factory, there were several people there, (ah well, pride comes before a fall) and I asked if I might use their phone to ring the AA.

Apparently, I had run out of petrol – how embarrassing! I could deal with the broken tooth but I could not deal with admitting I'd run out of petrol. I said as much to the AA man. The nice AA man lifted the bonnet and talked me through what 'fault' I could say had caused the breakdown. I lied through my teeth – so to speak – and never did admit to running out of petrol to anyone – until now!

I didn't get to the dentist that day, and I lost count of the number of staff and visitors coming to our enquiries desk singing, 'All I Want for Christmas is my Two Front Teeth' and 'Fangs for the Memory'.

May 1977

Around this time I had a birthday and decided to drive us out to the country and have tea somewhere the children could have a romp around. I knew the very place – Blakeshay Farm, Ulverscroft Lane, Newtown Linford. At that point I knew few people in that area and felt sure I would need to book, but there was no one to ask. Telephone directory – no entry under Blakeshay and I didn't know a surname to look under. I flicked through the directory and a page fell open at letter N and there I read: Neal, Blakeshay Farm. Now what are the chances of that happening? I booked and we spent a carefree afternoon. It wasn't a working farm but had the freedom for the children to run wild for a while. Blakeshay is no longer a tearoom and is privately owned, but what another wonderful memory.

I have a couple more strange-to-explain stories – but later.

***

June 1977 – The Queen's jubilee year

Now I had security, my own home, a mortgage, a car (box on wheels) a dog and, oh yes, three children, aged 14, 12 and 9.

The children settled happily into village life, particularly Danny, whose life was around animals – he was still bringing in the cows for Mr Sibson. One morning, at 4.30 a.m., he was told there was an inspector coming. What wasn't he told? It was April 1st!

He brought pigeons home from Melton Mowbray

market, who would fly off the next day, never to be seen again. Homing pigeons! Well trained!

A cockerel was taken back after a week as it woke the neighbours too early – and me!

And the final straw, having to set a trap for a pet mouse that was running up and down the water pipes on all three floors. We could smell mouse; and the final straw? Said mouse nibbled through the new lagging jacket for material for its nest. I'm very patient, and tolerant by nature, but enough is enough.

Rachel had best friends now, but she also had a few problems from a small group of girls. Rae had beautiful, thick, shoulder-length hair, and a school trip to the theatre had Rae distraught – those same girls had thrown chewing gum down from the upper circle into her hair - what a mess! But we had a cunning plan.

We had to cut the chewing gum out and then wash and restore her hair. Off to school the next morning, Rae was all smiles and said absolutely nothing. Troublemakers like attention – they must have been disappointed that day and never bothered her again.

Matt was growing into a character, what he didn't know he made up, and exaggerated massively. Nevertheless, Matt was happy, likeable and popular – a lovable rogue, and at 52, nothing has changed!

***

You may well ask, what has all this to do with 39 jobs? With a growing family there was always too much month at the end of the money.

I had a spare bedroom and a friend of mine had a friend looking for lodgings for two to three months. I became a landlady again. Luckily, no cooked breakfasts required.

In May 1977 our new lodger, Brian, moved in with his cat, at around 12.30 p.m., lunchtime, and by 1.30 p.m. he was off to play cricket leaving me with a rather unsettled cat. I daren't let it out, it might get lost, so I spent all afternoon trying to settle the cat – food, drink, shut him in his master's bedroom (familiar smells, I thought). This went on until 10.00 p.m. when said lodger returned, walked through the front door with, wait for it, *his* cat under his arm, while the poor cat I had mistakenly imprisoned made its escape. It must have been a neighbour's cat, who had wandered in while my lodger was moving in. I never saw that cat again – I cannot think why!

Brian coming to lodge with us only happened because someone else's life changed. Brian and his wife had separated and were awaiting a divorce and for the sale of their property in Markfield.

Brian's close friend Keith, and Keith's fiancé, had also split up and Brian was lodging with Keith until he, Brian, could get his own place – are you with me so far?

After some months Keith's fiancé returned – relationship on again and Brian needed to move out.

Brian was unknown to me but was a friend of a friend, and that was how he, and his cat, came to lodge with us for what was to have been around three months.

Brian, said lodger, was a sport and geography teacher at St Paul's RC School on Spencefield Lane in

Leicester, which was still Corpus Christi, Gwendolen Road, for another couple of years. He drove a gorgeous Triumph Spitfire sports car. If my rust bucket was out of action, he would throw me his car keys and off I would drive. That caused some speculation, I can tell you. Landlady, age difference, three children ...

Speculation can sometimes be correct, and this was so in our case.

Autumn 1977

Newtown Linford Cricket Club had a Ladies' Night held at the Bracken Hill Restaurant (Henry's place) dancing to Pogles Wood. It was a magical evening.

Brian asked his close friend, Des, to announce our engagement, taking everyone by surprise. When had Brian proposed? He never did – he asked me if I would consider adding to my family and following my favourable reply, with the proviso that the house, my lovely house, was too small and had no garden, Brian promptly started looking for a larger house for us all.

We were together for thirty-eight years. Fate or chance? I'm still pondering on that question.

***

A funny story

I think everyone was pleased, and relieved, that someone had charge of Brian; he was always being teased about his appearance: cricket whites now pink, trousers with creases pressed down the seams, general appearance in competition with Compo from Last of the Summer Wine ...

One particular evening in September, Brian's birthday, at the Cricket Club, I had given him new tops, he also had new trousers and looked smart.

At five minutes to midnight a group of his friends, without a word, picked Brian up and carried him out of the Club saying, 'we have to get him back into John Collier's window before midnight strikes.'

John Collier's – men's outfitters, advertised on TV with the slogan: 'John Collier, John Collier, the window to watch'.

***

Brian and I married in March 1978, having moved to a bigger house, and Rebecca Aimeé, Becky, was born in March 1979, two months before my fortieth birthday. Becky was quite a heavyweight – 10 lbs 4 oz – no c-section – ouch!

My pregnancy was not a good one and did my usual trick of nine months of sickness – very weakening for me, but not the baby – evidently!

***

Another funny story

I was eight months pregnant and craving salted peanuts. I kept a secret supply in a saucepan under the sink. With the children upstairs I decided to sneak a few nuts and, putting my hand into the pan and into the bag of nuts, I felt movement – I was touching a mouse's head and whiskers. I screamed! Danny, then 16, ran straight past me to fetch our neighbour thinking the baby was on its way.

It was scary, but so funny later.

... I was touching a mouse's head and whiskers...!

I did my best to keep working throughout my pregnancy – remember, conscientious, hard-working. To achieve this I spent my lunchtimes in the nurse's room, and providing there was a couch available, I slept for three-quarters of an hour. The sound of many feet pounding down the corridor to the shop, bank and canteen made no difference, I slept.

Usually, I would wake with no reminder (self-hypnosis) but occasionally the nurse would call me, and once, only once, Geoff rang to see if I was still there. And that's how I got through.

Liz had left by then and she and Tom were in Abu Dhabi in the Emirates for a couple of years and were to be Becky's godparents.

Danny, 16, Rae, 14, Matt, 11, and baby Becky, who was adored by us all.

I took a few months at home; Becky had a serious milk allergy, lactose intolerance, which needed careful monitoring. There were hospital stays and hospital appointments and she was 10 weeks old before she began to gain weight.

After a while, and needing to go back to work, we decided that I should work either evenings or weekends, thus assuring that one of us would be with Becky rather than using child care.

A council-owned, elderly people's home were advertising for weekend staff: full day Saturday one week, full day Sunday the following week; time-and-a-half pay on Saturdays, double pay on Sundays. Initially, I worked in the kitchen and later changed to night-shift duty on the care side.

I remember Matron – not my favourite person – being so mean to Draga, the cook, who I worked with in the kitchen. Draga and I still keep in touch after forty years.

A few interesting characters popped up at the home. Mostly young people serving community hours for shoplifting, GBH and other misdemeanours, would be sent to the home to serve their hours with us. One lad – were there Goths back in the 80s? – always dressed in black leather, big boots, etc. would put on an apron and work with the elderly residents. If a resident had had an accident, as in doubly-incontinent, he would willingly take them to the bathroom, clean them up, shower and re-dress them. He was a very caring young man. It taught me not to pre-judge.

In 1982 I was part of a team conducting a population census. I was nervous having been given Beaumont Leys, a fairly new area at that time. I had to knock on doors and often help with filling in the forms. Hostile? No. Hospitable? Amazingly so. Interesting people? Well, I'd say a witch's coven would count as interesting – they assured me they were good witches. Fascinating!

***

One slight problem as Becky began to speak – she would call her dad Bri. Bri, of course, wanted to be Daddy to Becky, so we asked my three if they would call Bri 'Daddy Bri' just until she got the idea. It worked beautifully, and in fact, Rae was to call him, and introduce him, as Daddy Bri from then on, and Becky called him Daddy.

Bri would always greet us with a kiss when he arrived home from school, then before anything else he would go upstairs to change. By this time of day, and now aged 40+, I was exhausted both mentally and physically by this active, never-stops-talking little dynamo. One day I said, 'Daddy, take this baby away from me,' meaning take her upstairs with you and give me a little break. For a time after that, Becky would run to Bri, arms outstretched to be picked up, and she would say, 'Daddy, Daddy, take this baby away from me!'

***

I left Abbey House in 1983 to open my own business – my dream: a dress shop for ladies 5ft 2in and under. Dresses scaled down to fit us little ladies, where a normal dress assumed the wearer to be 5ft 4in and the waist would land somewhere on our hips.

We called the shop, which we opened in Birstall, Simply Small.

Fashion Specialists for Ladies' 5'2" and under.
Sizes 8-24

√imply ∫mall

Proprietors:
BRIAN and GAY REDSTONE

Initially, we were very successful. Our 'little ladies' were travelling from all over the Midlands and an article in *Woman's Own* magazine was a great boost for us. But lack of capital to carry us through a cold, wet summer followed by a mild winter, affected the rag trade, particularly when specialist stock has to be pre-ordered before each season. The bankruptcy of a major stockist was also our downfall.

We sold Simply Small at a loss in 1986, and having honoured all of our debts to manufacturers, we were left broke for many years to come.

We were advised to declare bankruptcy, but we felt strongly that *that* was not an honourable way to go. Bankruptcy has such a knock-on effect on others, as we had experienced ourselves.

If there is a moral to this story it is this: Do as I say, not as I do. Never risk capital that you cannot afford to lose – think about it.

Regrets? Brian's take on it was: 'Babe, we shared the dream, we would have shared the success, so we would share the loss with no regrets and no recriminations.'

And that's how it was – no regrets, no recriminations.

What an amazing guy!

***

Another act of kindness

The day I opened Simply Small a very smart young lady, aged around 15, asked if I required a Saturday girl.

No, but if I did, Maria would be the first person I would call.

Within weeks Maria did become my Saturday girl, and being creative, she would often help me to re-dress the window display.

In 1985, Maria had left school, left Simply Small, and become a trainee hairdresser.

Sadly, that year my Danny died, suddenly and tragically, aged 21. Jenny, my able assistant, took over the shop for a while and Maria, now 17, would come in and re-dress the window for me without me asking, and giving up her own time. Such kindness; another lifelong friend.

Window display – that reminds me. One Christmas, Jenny, who was a brilliant seamstress, had made this beautiful, scaled-down cocktail dress in black and brights – it was part of the window display. A customer tried it on, fell in love with it, but couldn't decide. She came back two days later to purchase it, but sadly we had to tell her that it was sold. However, what we didn't add was that we had sold it to her husband, who made us promise not to say! She came to see us in the New Year to tell us all about the 'surprise'.

***

In the early 1980s I invested in another little business venture – I never give up. This was photo glazing, a method of cutting out and sticking photographs to plates, covering them with a liquid glaze and baking them in a special machine, which was about the size of a microwave. Baking took about thirty seconds and formed a skin over the photographs.

I was into photography at that time and took many photos of Bradgate Park, the deer, ducks, swans, flora and fauna, and sunsets.

I sold the plates at craft fairs and picked up orders for customers' own photographs to be photo glazed.

I remember a lady in Coalville who had a photograph

of her son with his pit pony outside a pit head. She told me that he was the last ostler to come out of that pit. I can't remember which pit, but one in the Coalville area.

And the lady in Rearsby – when I delivered a plate of her husband with his grandson, she showed me her collection of plates, which she had promised to do, all in shades of green, including a full dinner service of Mason Stoneware in Green Chartreuse – yes, she was Irish. I was telling her that I collected Mason Stoneware in Blue Manderley – all six pieces!

Photo glazing was not a lucrative business, but it helped pass the time as I waited for the shop to sell.

As always, I was meeting such interesting people.

The day Simply Small was sold and contracts signed was such a sad and depressing day for me. Brian still had his teaching career, I had nothing; somehow I had to start again.

Over the year that it took to sell Simply Small, the selling agent, Dilip Rajani, would drop by to keep me updated, and the kettle would go on.

Dilip's office was on London Road, Leicester, just above the train station. The fateful day arrived, Dilip took me to the buying agent's office and everything was signed over. We went back to Dilip's office, the kettle went on and Dilip offered me a job – part-time receptionist, coffee maker for his clients, and, oh yes, moving Dilip's car around London Road and side streets to avoid parking fines. Clearly a stop-gap for me.

I will always remember, on that day, how deflated and depressed I felt in the morning, but by 2.00 p.m. feeling elated and realising that whatever happened in my life, I would survive.

I appreciated what Dilip had done for me and after a short time I moved on. Dilip lives and works in London now.

***

After selling the shop and working with Dilip for a short time, I went back to County Hall, this time to the typing pool – me, dyslexic – typing pool?

The position was part-time on the audio dictation tape deck, cleaning the tapes on a machine that magnetically wiped the tapes blank ready to go out to the various departments throughout County Hall to be re-used. The office had at least thirty typists. My boss now was Mrs Chris Prattley, Geoff's wife, and it was the easiest job I ever had. It was time-share – mornings one week and afternoons the next – with one other person. We soon changed this to a two-and-a-half-day week each, which was a brilliant arrangement.

In theory, we should have been comfortably off, but because of Simply Small we had large debts to service, so still more month at the end of the money. Still looking to earn extra, I secured an evening job, possibly three evenings a week, at Security Express on Boston Road, Beaumont Leys, Leicester – a firm making-up cash wages for firms in the city (1980s). This was, for me, evening work, 6.00 p.m. – 11.00 p.m. Now I know I have this image of being prim and proper, and this image soon changes as you get to know me, but the girls I worked with, who were full-time, would always manage to get a shocked reaction from me. 'Tell Gay that joke,' or 'Tell Gay that story in last night's Leicester Mercury.'

'Oh my gosh,' or words to that effect, I would say, suitably shocked, at which point they would fall into peals of laughter – I never disappointed.

Sadly, one of the ladies had a grandson who was being treated for cancer, spending days in the children's ward at Leicester Royal Infirmary. I suggested that instead of Christmas cards to each other we give a donation to buy toys for that ward. A neighbour of mine in Anstey, Maureen, worked for Mattel Toys who promised to double the money we raised. We collected £40.00, which doubled to £80.00 and the money was spent on gifts for the ward, and for Ben himself.

Working evenings meant missing out on bedtimes with my youngest child, Becky, now around eight years old and at primary school. I would leave a note on Becky's pillow and would find her reply on my pillow on my return. We both loved these exchanges; she would sometimes ask me a question like, 'I cannot remember how to spell vanilla and it's coming up in a test.'

'Mum, I can't remember how to spell vanilla'

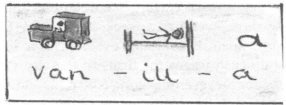

Easy!

I was actually made redundant, along with others – last in, first out. I don't recall a job where I have laughed so much – a brilliant group of girls!

Another story to lighten the mood

From the beginning of our relationship, Brian (Bri) called me Babe. You might think that I would object to this, but as I was six and a half years older than Bri, I found it quite acceptable. The fact was, he called many young people Babe – I must have been his special Babe.

Bri was a very popular teacher; funny but always had total control. Did I say 'always'?

Meeting Brian out of school one afternoon we, Becky and I, sat quietly at the back of the class, waiting for the lesson to end.

Suddenly: 'Daddy!'

'Yes, Babe.'

'Are these your babies?'

Did I say: 'Sir always has total control?' Not for the rest of that lesson! The class erupted, could not stop laughing, including 'Sir', who swiftly brought the lesson to a close.

From the mouths of babes ...

***

Goodbye sports car

By this time, Brian had said goodbye to his beloved Spitfire and had purchased a large Ford Estate. Six of us didn't fit into the Spitfire however hard we tried. We managed to get four of us in but getting four of us out was a different matter – sardines! Ford Estate family car put us back in the real world. The Spitfire was a fun car and we travelled far, often singing along to our favourite tape, *ABBA Gold*. Happy memories.

Let's catch up with the children

Daniel (Danny)

Danny continued to look out for old Mr Sibson even after the cows had been sold. Dan would pop in most days after school and make sure he was all right. One day he came home and told me Mr Sibson got tangled up with his braces and Dan had sorted out and threaded the braces back under Mr Sibson's jumper and tidied him up – what a picture!

Dan was heartbroken having been round one day and found the farmhouse locked up and Mr Sibson gone – into a care home, evidently – and no one had told Dan. We figured out that maybe no one knew of their friendship.

Another elderly friend was George King. Danny would often be seen riding around the village with George in George's pony and trap. George was widowed and definitely not into cleaning; Dan would come home and tell us that he had, 'spring cleaned George's kitchen.'

Danny was so caring but he was 'different' and had major issues to deal with. Danny was transgender (female in a male body) and this came to a head at around five years old. We had gone to a summer fete at a large house on London Road in Leicester. We'd lost Danny and when he was found he was in a nearby garden clutching a doll, taken from one of the stalls – a beautiful doll with long hair. The doll was returned, but once back home I sat down with him and made a plan. A doll similar to the one he had run off with would cost around £5.00, so Dan was to earn pocket money to £2.50 at which point I would double it, and if he still wanted a doll then we would go and buy one. Interestingly, the new doll had long brunette hair and Dan washed, brushed, curled and trimmed it until eventually, after two–three years, the hair was all gone and the doll dispensed with.

There were critics who thought I was wrong to encourage him, but I think I was accepting what was obvious and have never regretted what I did.

Danny struggled at school, purposely missing the school bus and walking to school – Anstey to Quorn, Rawlins, arriving at around 11.30 a.m. in time for lunch break. Being a part-time student suited Dan very well, but the reality was that contact sports were too much for him to cope with – football, rugby, hockey. Yet he was very good at swimming, diving, skiing, horse riding – all the non-contact sports.

Dan had his own pony. His love of all animals, great and small, was for many years his salvation.

This isn't the place to tell the whole story. Dan and Rae were devoted siblings. Dan now 6ft tall to Rae's 5ft 2in, they would go around together arm in arm. Dan would occasionally cross-dress and with make-up would look stunning.

Dan always hoped for a transgender operation, which he was deemed not stable enough to deal with, and in May 1985, aged 21, he took his own life.

A shocking waste of a beautiful, kind and caring young person.

Rachel (Rae)

Rae, like her brother, loved Anstey and made many friends, Lorraine becoming a lifelong friend.

At sixteen, Rae left school and enrolled on a two-year Catering and Management course at Southfields College, now Leicester College. Rae found the course hard and the lecturers moving along too fast; she believed she wasn't going to cope.

Bri and I sat down with her and asked her to stay with the course for one term and if she felt she still wasn't coping then we would help her to change to another course.

In the meantime, we felt that if Rae was struggling then so were some of the other students. What we persuaded her to do was to be really brave, raise her hand and say, 'I'm sorry, you're moving along so fast I cannot absorb all the information.'

She did that the following day, the lecturer apologised and immediately slowed down. After class, Rae was surrounded by other students saying, 'Good on you, we felt the same and dare not say!'

At the end of the two-year course Rae was one of the top three students who were given the opportunity to go to America for a four-month work experience – another life-changing event.

The three students flew out to Albany, New York

State, 180 miles from New York City, working for a hotel chain. They worked very hard, as you do in catering, but what an amazing experience. They played hard too and made many friends.

A few months after returning home and planning to go to teacher training college, Rae returned to Albany to say, 'Hi' to everyone, met Mike, who she hadn't met previously, and only came home for a few days to tell us that she and Mike were to marry and she would live in America. Quite a shock for us, but we were happy for her. They married in April 1985, when Rae was twenty.

Danny was in hospital and devastated not to be well enough to go to the wedding. I decided to stay home with him and Rae understood my reasons. It was a very hard decision but the right one. Sadly it was six weeks later that Danny left us.

Rae had a wonderful life in America. Mike made a promise that she would come to England once a year to see us all, and he kept that promise.

They had a large circle of friends and life was good. But Rachel never got over Danny's death and we believe that the medication given for a breakdown caused Rae to become bi-polar.

Bi-polar is not the same as depression; you can be living a 'normal' life and suddenly go either very 'high' or sink into a black hole of despair. Some of the medication that was given to Rae was later taken off the market.

During the twenty years in America Rae had three of these episodes, the first one a year after her marriage – 1986. She got over that and had two beautiful daughters, Abigail and Emily. She was a wonderful mother – happy, no sign of illness, then, when the girls were six and four, Rae had her second bi-polar episode, ending up in a psychiatric hospital, eventually going forward again. The medication was so good we, and she, believed the condition could be controlled for the foreseeable future.

Life was good again and then totally unexpectedly and almost overnight, another bi-polar episode, another black hole. Abigail was thirteen and Emily, eleven. This was too much for our lovely girl, who didn't want her girls to see her like that, and in October 2005, aged forty, Rae left us to go to Danny.

Why is life so cruel?

***

I learnt something that has been a great help to me over the years:

> *It is only possible to hold one thought at a time.*
> *Therefore, you can change a negative thought*
> *into a positive one.*
> *You are in control.*
> *It works!*

Matthew (Matt)

Let's catch up with Matt.

Matt, at around 3 years old, was affectionately labelled 'a lovable rogue'. Cheeky, funny, lovable, generous – he'd give you his last Rolo, and at 52 that description still fits.

Matt hated school, never studied and never bothered to collect exam results, but to his credit, the day he left he found a job, even stopping people in the street to tell them!

Matt is father to six children and granddad to four.

Some years ago, he traced his birth mother, but didn't keep in touch. Later, I met Dianne myself and we have become close friends.

Rebecca (Becky)

I haven't said a lot about Becky; I guess that's because she has never been a problem.

Her milk allergy continued until she was eleven – we got used to reading every label.

Becky sailed through school and from high school onwards she saw school as a social event, a place to have a fun time with friends, with just enough studying.

We asked why this group of girls was not split up.

'Oh, no, they're such lovely girls, we wouldn't consider splitting them up.'

Now in their forties, and with children of their own, they are still close friends and full of fun.

The same group on an upper school trip to Germany spent evenings in a local bar (best not to ask what they drank). A German bar? No, Paddy's Irish bar. We have Irish bars in Leicester – we could have saved money!

Leaving school, Becky did a two-year nursery nurse's course – NNEB – at Leicester College. She was very successful and has worked with children ever since.

She lives in Anstey with fiancé, Daren, and their children, Logan, 10 and Amber, 7, and I count my blessings that I agreed to add to my family.

I used to worry that Becky might not want to be seen out with an 'older' mum, but that has never been the case and over the years we have done many fun things together.

***

I am nanna to ten grandchildren and five great-grandchildren.

PART 4

New skills

Starting a new skill – rush seating

I was always interested in country crafts, and a follower of the Arts and Crafts movement, and a friend, Johnnie Richardson, was making Shaker style furniture – rocking chairs, carver and dining chairs. Beautifully crafted, the chairs had to be rush seated and Johnnie needed help with this. Because of my interest, I wondered if I could pick up the skill of this style of seating and took myself off to a Saturday, one-day course, for rush seating. After attending I had doubts about this course as it left a few people with half-finished chairs and not enough rush or skill to finish them.

Case in point, a quite elderly couple took two kitchen chairs and later went home with two, now unusable, kitchen chairs. We had become friends by the end of the day, as you do, and I promised them that if I took up the craft, then I would contact them.

I started working for Johnnie, and through practise, practise and more practise, became a skilled rush seater.

Several months later I contacted my 'new' friends and re-seated the chairs for them. They related this fascinating story to me:

Their son was to be married; a successful business man he had recently purchased The Hall in Old Dalby. My friends, wanting to buy a suitable wedding gift, decided they would visit antique shops in Rutland – a different town each Monday. The first Monday's visit was to Uppingham and the first antique shop they came to was displaying a beautiful fender in the window. They went into the shop for further investigation. They began talking to the assistant who said, 'I'm not trying to do a hard sell, but the fender has a matching companion set, may I show it to you?' The rest, as they say, is history. After purchasing the items the assistant asked where they were being taken. 'The Hall, Old Dalby,' they replied. Silence. Then, 'That's where they came from,' he said!

I continued to rush seat all of Johnnie's chairs; at first in a shed at the back of their cottage. Johnnie's wife, Lyn, an artist, was a close friend of mine and later worked alongside Johnnie when he moved across to a workshop in one of the stables at Beach Farm in Newtown Linford. To me, a country girl, it was a wonderful environment; the smell of the wood (ash) that Johnnie steam-bent, and the damp rush, I loved. As for Johnnie, a true craftsman who loved to chat. Friends would pop by and that was the excuse. 'Put the kettle on, gel.' I knew my place. An hour later he would still be talking away, no pressure, not a care in the world.

Johnnie had had a wonderful childhood. Bradgate Park was his playground; his father a gardener, his mother a housekeeper, both working for the Gimson family at Stoneywell, that beautiful house, which is now a National Trust property.

I often went to craft fairs with Johnnie, he would have a stand and I would demonstrate rush seating while Johnnie would beeswax a chair he had made, and basically talk! To be fair, he did get orders for his chairs.

Eventually, I set up my own workshop at home as I had begun to take in repair work, re-seating old chairs privately. I had also taught myself, from books, how to cane-seat and that was bringing in plenty of work for me, but I continued to seat Johnnie's chairs.

"Country Seat"

RUSH AND CANE SEATING

Gay Redstone

Rush and Cane Seat Restoration

To work with rush it has to be prepared the day before and my last task, therefore, was to get my supply ready for the next day. I would lay an old sheet on the patio or the lawn, select the amount of rush needed for the next day, fill a watering can and soak the rush, wrap it up and leave it overnight, it is then soft and pliable and ready to work with.

I usually did rush seating in the evening as I worked other jobs during the day, picking up with The Archers again after a thirty-year gap and remembering some of the characters – the twins, Kenton and Shula, now grown up. My day ended around 8.30 p.m. when Brian would come and tell me dinner would be on the table, with a glass of wine, in fifteen minutes, which gave me time to prepare the next day's rush – teamwork!

I was lucky enough to get a call from Don and Ann Gimson to collect and re-rush their kitchen chairs, and Don took me round their beautiful home showing me also a record book of the cost of rush seating a chair – 2/6d (12½p) back in the 1930s.

Tony Handley of Oxford harvested the rush from Oxfordshire rivers, both for his own business and for sale. He would visit me once a year with my supply of rush and on one occasion, when watching me work, he said, 'I would never employ you, your work is beautiful but you're too slow.' Thanks, Tony. I decided to take that as a compliment but it did explain why I never got rich being a bottomer (rush seater). My friend Johnnie lives on a narrowboat now and my dear friend Lyn died several years ago. Lyn was well known locally as an animal artist, and her interest in river boat art of the bargees – castles and roses. A very interesting couple.

***

Talking about crafts and furniture brings another amazing story.

In 2002, Broughtons, the iron mongers, relocated to the old cinema in Anstey from Leicester. Apart from ironmongery they sold small items of furniture along with gifts and soft furnishings. I spent a lot of time there. One such visit I fell in love with a nest of tables – oval, polished oak – and after several more visits I purchased them. We had a large lounge and needed another coffee table. Brian had an idea – back to Broughton's with a question: would they sell me just the large table from an identical set?

The answer, obviously, 'No'.

Returning to the showroom several weeks later and wandering around drooling over all the lovely items, I happened to overhear a conversation between a young couple and an assistant.

'We love this nest of tables,' the young man was saying, 'but the large table of the set is too big for our small lounge. Would it be possible to purchase just the two smaller tables?'

The answer, obviously, 'No.'

'Excuse me,' I chipped in, 'I overheard your conversation. I'm interested in just the large table of the set. If we could agree on splitting the cost, could we purchase them between us?'

Five minutes later, price agreed, tables paid for, deal done; three very happy customers carrying out their purchases, leaving behind one slightly bemused sales assistant probably wondering what had just happened.

Now, what are the chances of me being in that showroom, that day, that hour, that moment, passing by that group of people having that conversation?

This is absolutely true, and sometimes, just sometimes, fact is stranger than fiction.

***

Maplewell Hall School, 1989 to 1993

I secured a place at Maplewell Hall Special School, in Woodhouse Eaves, as a classroom assistant, specifically to work with Ben, a special needs pupil. A happy school but with learning difficulties also came behavioural problems.

Ben was in a class with eight other pupils. He was always a delight to work with – the original happy chappie. He had an amazing musical ear, could play the piano without, I believe, ever having had a lesson, and could tell purely through listening that the school piano had been tuned – apparently just the previous day when we enquired!

Ben never stopped smiling; it would take him forever just to pick up his pencil to write his name. Ben would look at me and say, 'Mrs Redstone cross with Ben,' and he would go off into peals of laughter. Me, cross? Never. Frustrated? Perhaps a little.

Something I found really interesting: These children were learning French and studying Shakespeare albeit at a very basic level. By contrast, I left secondary modern education in 1954 without being given the opportunity to learn French or to study Shakespeare. Were we not considered bright enough? Christine and Coralie were amazing teachers and I was always involved with the whole class.

An amusing story: A non-uniform day and a school walk around the Loughborough Outwoods. Ben is happily walking with a group ahead of me. Wayne, from Ben's class, is walking along arm in arm with me. He has learning difficulties but is streetwise. Wayne is twelve years old.

'Mrs Redstone,'

'Yes, Wayne.'

'Can I call you by your first name just for today?'

'Yes, Wayne. Just for today. My name is Gay.'

Silence from Wayne while he absorbed this information and then, 'That's unfortunate isn't it miss?' and he continued to call me Mrs Redstone. How hilarious is that?

I loved my time at Maplewell Hall. Ben, now a teenager, was a delight to work with, as was all his classmates who, even with their varied problems, you grew to love.

However, it was time to move on.

***

I am now going to go quickly through several jobs before following on from Maplewell Hall. They are not in order but were part of that period of time, 1980s/1990s.

Taxi driving

I applied and took an exam to hold a taxi cab licence. The exam entailed knowledge – not **The** Knowledge the London cabbies have to take – of local city and county of Leicestershire. This I knew pretty well through working at Richmond House School clinic. I didn't altogether enjoy this job and early on realised that there were too may cabbies trying to earn an honest crust, and some were the only breadwinners. So, although our needs were also great, I did feel uneasy and left them to it.

Selling health insurance to farmers

Away for one week's training and I was – in a word – hopeless! Dyslexia does not lend itself to memorising rebuttals. I left just one week after the training. The most stressful job I ever had!

The Cambridge Diet

Again, no dates. I became a slimming adviser for the Cambridge Diet, that is, drinks, snack bars, slimming plans – a highly successful diet, if you follow it properly.

County Hall again

Now, I don't know how, why or when, but I found myself back working in County Hall, Glenfield's telephone exchange – two full-time staff and me, part-time. I cannot remember how long I stayed but it was in the 1980s.

Double glazing

I enjoyed the training, drawing and measuring, and started selling. We were given small orders to start with, probably a kitchen door and window, or a new front door – £1,000, give or take. This particular day I went to measure for what we understood to be a small order and went back to the office with a £4,000, whole-house order – a lot of money in the 1990s. Unfortunately, I had made an error in as much as the windows all had stone sills, which added £400 for the extra work needed. I had earned £400 in commission on that one order and of course expected to lose some of that commission. In their wisdom they took the whole £400 off me, which I felt wasn't very wise and certainly not encouraging. I soon moved on.

Southfields College (now Leicester College)

For a short time I was an invigilator at the college, covering for staff on sick leave. I really enjoyed that.

***

About all the jobs: Close friends, Janet and Ray live in Hertfordshire; Ray worked in the city and is now retired. I remember saying to Ray, 'I guess you wouldn't employ me given my record.'

'As a matter of fact, I would,' he replied. 'You wouldn't be set in your ways, you would be adaptable, teachable and obviously a team player. I would hope to keep you more than four years, but yes, I would employ you.'

I think that may go on my headstone (the one I'm not planning to have) – 'she was adaptable'.

***

1993–97 Traveller Education

I still wanted to work with children and was accepted in a post at Traveller Education. My remit was to support two teachers who travelled around city schools working with traveller, fairground and circus children as they passed through the city, and also the children from Meynell's Gorse, a permanent traveller site in Braunstone. Originally the base was a double mobile unit in the grounds of The Martin High School,

Anstey, but sadly burnt to the ground around 1995; an accident. As a temporary base we moved to Beaumanor Hall in Woodhouse, in a wooden structure in the grounds of this beautiful hall. They are now based at Beaumont Lodge, Astill Lodge Road, Leicester.

I spent a lot of my time at Braunstone Frith Primary School, working with 5–11 year olds, mostly children from Meynell's Gorse, teaching them to read and often going to Meynell's Gorse to follow up if children were absent.

Traveller girls rarely attended school after 10 years of age, staying to look after siblings and keeping them away from non-traveller boys.

Another of my amusing stories

A Braunstone Frith trip to the Haymarket Theatre for a Christmas production, and sharing my sweets with the children around me, Jim-boy, sitting next to me, suddenly offered me his half-eaten, or should I say chewed, Curly Wurly.

''Av a bite of this, miss.'

'Thanks for offering, Jim-boy, but no, thank you.'

'Goo on, miss.'

'No, you enjoy it, dear.'

'Goo on, miss, you gev me some of yourn, and we 'av to share, you said.'

'Thank you, Jim-boy,' and closing my eyes, I took a bite.

Jim was the first in his whole family to read and write – he was 8 years old.

***

Mellor Primary, Checketts Road, Leicester, was another school I spent a lot of time at.

Fairground children, two brothers, who came into their 'winter yard' (Bath Street) from late autumn until early spring, came into Mellor Primary – a lovely school with first names being used for teachers and pupils alike. It really worked – absolutely no lack of respect. It was by far my favourite school.

I rarely worked with Penny and Fran, the teachers I supported; mostly they would introduce me to the headmaster, school secretary, etc. and leave me to do the job.

One most interesting time at Mellor was working with five children from the Moscow State Circus. They spoke only a little English but we got by. My remit was to support the class teachers. One little chap, a five-year old, didn't want to do his sums until his seven-year-old cousin whispered something into his ear and he immediately settled down to work.

'What did you say to him?' I asked.

He said, 'I told him he would not grow strong to be a trapeze artist like his mum and dad if he didn't do his sums.' Now I thought that applied to eating your greens, your 'veggie troubles' as my friend Geraldine (Gerry) called them.

Jennia, the ringmaster's daughter and probably around ten years old, was the leader of the group and quite bossy. Leaving Leicester after a couple of weeks I bought little gifts for them, the two girls and three boys: little ruler, pencil and rubber sets, blue for boys, mauve for the girls. Jennia asked, 'Why you give boys nice present and girls not nice present?' Honestly, they were so similar. I gently took the gift from her, put it to one side and said, 'No problem, I will give the gift to another girl in your class who will love it.' The gift disappeared – Jennia took it home with her.

One afternoon after school I went with Fran to the 'Big Top' in Abbey Park, and watched Jennia practising on the tightrope, which was about one metre off the ground. Presumably it had started lower and would be raised, little by little. What a different lifestyle to most other children, and very disciplined.

The day they left Mellor after two weeks was very emotional. One little boy cried and hugged me and kept running back and hugging me. These little ones spend a good part of their lives saying, 'goodbye'.

***

Back to the Travellers

Appleby Fair was a yearly event for the traveller community. Thousands of Gypsy, Traveller and Romany families meet in Appleby in Westmoreland, Cumbria, for a five-day gathering. I was able to go along a couple of years and it was quite an education! Non-food shops closed and boarded-up their shop fronts, restaurants and eateries stayed open and hoped to make a lot of money, which they would, without being trashed, which they might.

Mostly, Appleby is about buying and selling horses, wheeling and dealing, and what a sight to see: horses and ponies in the river being ridden, shampooed and groomed ready for sale – fifty or more at any one time. Love them or hate them, a fascinating group of people. I loved my time working with Travellers.

***

Around this time in 1995, and still wanting to rid ourselves of debt, we became interested in multi-level marketing (MLM). Starting badly, and not finding the right company, our first experience of MLM was disastrous – it cost us and made us more broke.

To make money in MLM, or Network Marketing, there has to be an affordable product to sell to the public, with repeat orders. With the first company the product was so expensive we were buying it ourselves, but no one else was.

We paid for meetings, conferences, compulsory-to-buy monthly books, bought £400's worth of make-up for Party Plan. It didn't take too long to see that it was us poor (stupid?) distributers who were making the fat-cats fatter.

However, 'The Books' were to change our lives – self-development books taught us a new way of thinking.

Now, Bri believed totally in building a network but realised it would only work with a saleable product.

Move on!

***

Kleeneze 1997

A leaflet dropped onto the mat. Becky, for holiday money, asked her dad what he thought of it.

Kleeneze: Seeking distributors with opportunity to team build (door to door catalogue distribution).

Becky wasn't really interested, but Brian immediately saw the potential. We both knew the catalogue well and over the years had been customers ourselves.

At this point in my memoir I remembered that this had been one of many jobs – a Kleeneze distributor, and I had a small customer base in Rothley – at that time not a Network Marketing Company; that was back in 1979, it is now 1997, eighteen years later.

We joined the company; Brian became a 'hoody', hoping not to see people we knew – a teacher putting catalogues through doors didn't sit comfortably at first. Of course, he bumped into some of his mates who uttered some rather colourful expletives, so the hood was taken off and he got on with the job. I joined him – I was now doing three part-time jobs.

By the autumn of 1997 I left the other jobs to concentrate on Kleeneze. At last we had found the right vehicle.

An interesting aside

We attended a meeting held by one of the upline (the person who signed us in). He stated, 'If a customer orders only one item at, say, £1.99, just ignore it; they're wasting your time.'

Later, when we left the meeting we looked at each other and said, 'We are on our own.' We believed that the £1.99 order was as important as a £99.00 order – our belief was to simply look after people and for them to trust us. The £1.99 orders soon became regular £10.00–£25.00 orders.

In the year 2000, aged 55, Brian took early retirement from his teaching career. He was by now a Head of Year to 200 sixteen-year-olds and loving it, but not liking the way teaching was changing.

We concentrated totally on Kleeneze and became team leaders, travelling all around Britain, Brian teaching self-development and self-belief, always accompanied by his wit and sense of humour. So many new friends in far-flung places: Devon, Cornwall, Wales, Lancashire, Scotland and, of course, Leicester.

Brian's teaching rubbed off on me and I became a speaker myself, getting an unheard of standing ovation for my talk to 300 distributors. 'If I can, you can.'

Kleeneze became our lives.

We won all-expenses-paid conferences (holidays) in amazing places. Monaco, Monte Carlo, Cairns, Australia and Sun City, South Africa.

Finally our lives had turned around. We were now debt free; it took fourteen years. No regrets, no recriminations and sheer hard work.

Certainly our characters were strengthened and we learnt never to give up.

Did we look after people? The 600 customers in Anstey, who became our friends, says we must have done. We were certainly well known in the village.

'It's the Kleenex lady!'

'Mam, it's the Betterware man!'

Dogs became our friends and they didn't have to remember our titles.

We loved what we did and eventually retired from Kleeneze in 2009; I was 70.

My working life had spanned fifty-five years.

Brian

Another devastating loss; my lovely husband, Brian passed away in 2016, five years after having a massive stroke in 2011, which left him unable to walk or care for himself.

Brian, that gentle giant, funny, caring, positive, always a happy character, and – oh yes, so laid back it was amazing he could stay upright! A bachelor at heart, totally unaware that lawns should be cut and cars should be cleaned, and, 'why would you want to decorate that room, Babe? It was only done twenty-five years ago!' But, he was the one person who, without doubt, encouraged me to believe in myself after a difficult upbringing. He taught me not to take life seriously – have fun! Given a crisis, Bri was there; a tower of strength, a rock, taking control – you relied on him totally. Crisis over and he went back to allowing everything to happen around him again.

Life was for living; don't look back, don't worry about tomorrow, live for today, live in the moment. In fact, it was impossible to quarrel with Bri and believe me, I tried. He would say, 'Why go on about that? That was yesterday, that's history.'

Brian started his teaching career at Corpus Christi, which later changed and became St Paul's Catholic School on Spencefield Lane in Evington where he stayed until his retirement. He taught PE and geography and in later years, careers, and was Head of Year 11. He took school skiing trips abroad for many years, and later water sports trips.

In the 70s and 80s, and long before 'Proms' came to us from America, Bri and the staff would take pupils to the Grand Hotel for a dinner dance – teaching etiquette and dress code. I can see them now; every girl wore black and looked gorgeous. At Christmas the same group would serve dinner and provide entertainment for local pensioners brought into the school and the young people did the shopping and set up the tables – the school cooks did the cooking. What wonderful life skills – I hope it became part of their memory bank.

Although we struggled financially for so long, being broke didn't stop us having fun and socialising. Summer took care of itself – cricket. And for me, unpaid labour helping Becky with the cricket teas – a good little earner for Becky.

We made our own wine from the hedgerows, very often with friends coming round we would syphon some off directly from the demijohn into jugs. For Becky's christening we made rose petal wine – a delicate pink – beautiful.

For over twenty years Christmas Eve was open house – very much a 'bring your own drink', plus our demijohns, and I would make mince pies and sausage rolls; nothing fancy or expensive, but so successful.

Towards Christmas Eve 1999 a neighbour asked, would we consider instead of Christmas Eve would we do a Millennium Eve? Thanks, Roger! We did both.

Millennium was special as Rae, Mike and the girls came over – what a night! Feasting, fireworks, friendships and fun.

So that was life with Brian; he was initially a lodger – one of my many jobs – he came for three months and stayed for thirty-eight years!

Thank you, Bri for thirty-eight fun-filled, amazing years. You added massively to my memoir.

My birth mother

It was Brian who helped me to find my birth mother. During the summer holidays in 1979 (Becky was five months old) Bri suggested we drive over to Sleaford in Lincolnshire, where I was born, and go to the council offices and ask to see the electoral register, which we did. We didn't find the name we were looking for, Rose ––, but we found the name Violet ––. We felt there could be a connection. Further enquiries led us to Horace ––, who was brother to Rose and Violet. Horace worked at the council offices and the office clerk knew him! Small world. Cutting a long story short, we had arrived at Sleaford around 11.00 a.m. and by 2.00 p.m. we were sitting with my 'mum' in her house. Amazing! And something else amazing, we had never met again after I went into care at six weeks old – forty years earlier – how come on that day, we were wearing the exact same outfits, only the colours differed!

We had ten years together, the last five Mum lived with us (she had been widowed one year before we met).

Life had been terribly hard for Mum, until, at forty-two, she married Bob. I found a half-brother and two half-sisters. All have died now, but I feel so blessed, as were my children, to have had them in our lives.

Perhaps I should write Mum's life story?

A price to pay

I learnt to drive when I was thirty-four, which enabled me to accept jobs off the beaten track, for example, Maplewell School, Beaumanor Hall, Traveller

Education, Langrop Garage, etc, so driving has been a great asset over the years. I have always loved driving, so imagine my shock when in 2019, aged eighty, I had my licence revoked! A shock even though, because of Parkinson's, I knew it was going to happen eventually.

To end on a lighter note, here is the poem I wrote at the time.

There is a Price to Pay

They have stopped me driving,
and this is what they say:
'Dear Madam, the DVLA regret to inform you,
we have taken your licence away.'

'Dear Madam,' indeed, how dare they?
I will still drive – a quitter I am not,
I will get myself a broomstick,
a witch's hat, and a cat.

My broomstick may not be of the conventional kind,
the style you would expect to see.
But, trust me when I tell you,
it will be suitable for me.

First, the DVLA will hear from me,
(oh yes, there is a price to pay).
Scaring them will be my mission;
they will regret what they took away!

I will land outside our village store,
filling customers with fear.
Top up my shopping trolley,
then simply disappear.

So I plan to 'stick' around some –
lots to celebrate, be sure of that.
The fun we will have scaring folk,
me, my broomstick, hat and cat!

In reality, my new mobility scooter is to be named
'The Broomstick'.

We come to the end of my journey. I promised it would not be boring and I hope that was correct.

This was to be a light-hearted memoir, but sadness happens and becomes part of the story, but you stayed with me, and mostly it has been fun.

Thank you for travelling with me.

Gay

ACKNOWLEDGEMENTS

George and Amanda Ballentyne and Kerry Walton who read my earlier attempts and encouraged me to continue.

Maxine Linnell and Rothley writers for their friendship and support.

Alan Veale, author and friend, thank you for your patience answering all my questions.

Dr Karen Ette who managed to format, edit and make sense of my dyslexia.

Sarah Houldcroft at Goldcrest Books who guided me through the publishing maze.

Thank you all.